RAMADAN IS BURNISHED SUNLIGHT

other books by the author

POETRY
Dawn Visions
Burnt Heart/Ode to the War Dead
This Body of Black Light Gone Through the Diamond
The Desert is the Only Way Out
The Chronicles of Akhira
The Blind Beekeeper
Mars & Beyond
Laughing Buddha Weeping Sufi
Salt Prayers
Ramadan Sonnets
Psalms for the Brokenhearted
I Imagine a Lion
Coattails of the Saint
Abdallah Jones and the Disappearing-Dust Caper
Love is a Letter Burning in a High Wind
The Flame of Transformation Turns to Light
Underwater Galaxies
The Music Space
Cooked Oranges
Through Rose Colored Glasses
Like When You Wave at a Train and the Train Hoots Back at You
In the Realm of Neither
The Fire Eater's Lunchbreak
Millennial Prognostications
You Open a Door and it's a Starry Night
Where Death Goes
Shaking the Quicksilver Pool
The Perfect Orchestra
Sparrow on the Prophet's Tomb
A Maddening Disregard for the Passage of Time
Stretched Out on Amethysts
Invention of the Wheel
Sparks Off the Main Strike
Chants for the Beauty Feast
In Constant Incandescence
Holiday from the Perfect Crime
The Caged Bear Spies the Angel
The Puzzle
Ramadan is Burnished Sunlight / Poems 2011

THEATER / THE FLOATING LOTUS MAGIC OPERA COMPANY
The Walls Are Running Blood
Bliss Apocalypse

PROSE
Zen Rock Gardening
The Little Book of Zen
Zen Wisdom

RAMADAN
IS BURNISHED SUNLIGHT

AUGUST 1 - 30, 2011
1 RAMADAN - 30 RAMADAN 1432

DANIEL ABDAL-HAYY MOORE

THE ECSTATIC EXCHANGE
2011
PHILADELPHIA

Ramadan is Burnished Sunlight / Poems 2011
Copyright © 2011 Daniel Abdal-Hayy Moore
All rights reserved.
Printed in the United States of America

For quotes any longer than those for critical articles and reviews, contact:
The Ecstatic Exchange,
6470 Morris Park Road, Philadelphia, PA 19151-2403
email: abdalhayy@danielmoorepoetry.com

First Edition
ISBN: 978-0-578-09246-1
Published by *The Ecstatic Exchange*,
6470 Morris Park Road, Philadelphia, PA 19151-2403

Also available from The Ecstatic Exchange:
Knocking from Inside, poems by Tiel Aisha Ansari

Acknowledgments: These poems in their entirety were first published on my poetry blog, www.ecstaticxchange.wordpress.com, each night of Ramadan 2011, with MP3 readings. For a CD of these readings, if not included in this copy, contact the author: abdalhayy@danielmoorepoetry.com.

Cover painting by Malika Moore
Back cover photograph by Malika Moore

DEDICATION

To
Shaykh ibn al-Habib (may Allah be pleased with him)
(and the continuation of the Habibiyya)
Shaykh Bawa Muhaiyuddeen,
all shuyukh of instruction and ma'arifa,
all those having fasted this Ramadan and
all Ramadans to come

and
Baji Tayyaba Khanum
of the unsounded depths

———

*The earth is not bereft
of Light*

CONTENTS

Author's Introduction   8

First Night of Ramadan   11
Four Corners of the Universe   13
Adam Stood in the World   15
Leave the World Alone   17
Black Cow Ramadan   18
A Flourish of Time   20
A Fiery Glow in the Heart   21
Splendid Excitement of the Coming Day   23
The Things of this World   25
Ramadan is Burnished Sunlight   26
His Pure Presence   28
Ramadan's Flame Hoops   30
Signs of Allah   33
Ramadan Goes Looking   35
Hand of Light   38
Halfway Through the Fast   40
The Capitulation of King Stomach   42
A Spider's Break-Fast   46
Extend Your Shadow   48
With a Two-Legged Goat and a Flying Fish   50
Ramadan Suns Itself   52
Pinpoint and Compass Point   55
Fast   57
Heart & Soul   58
Ramadan is a Gorgeous Chorus   60
If We Woke Up One Morning   62
Blue Circles   64

Nighttime Sessions of Light 66
The Repetitions of Saints 68
Irene 70
At the Pivot End of a Life 72
Elusive Crescent 75
A Sandwich at Noon 77

INDEX 81

AUTHOR'S INTRODUCTION

The Ramadan of August, 2011 (or 1432 by the lunar Islamic reckoning) was unique in many ways. It began with a heat wave, in Philadelphia where I live, and God in His Mercy lowered the temperatures overnight, and sent rain throughout the month to cool down the days. And the days were very long, about sixteen hours of fasting from dawn to sundown, but of course became shorter as the month wore on. This at first was a concern for my wife, Malika, and me, advancing in years (early 70s), and remembering the first Ramadans of our lives as Muslims over thirty years ago when the summer duration was roughly the same, but our youth more resilient. Or so it worried our minds. Then there was an *earthquake* in Philadelphia! Mild, but no occurrence of such an anomaly since around 1968, and supposed to be very rare, though not so upsetting in itself for me, having grown up in Oakland, California. And finally, Hurricane Irene, which sent a panic through the East Coast towns and cities, and was slated to cause, and did cause some horrific damage with high winds and slashing rains. It did rain for 40 days and 40 nights in one night it seemed, but our house remained snug and flood-free after all. An eventful Ramadan for sure. Still, at the beginning of it, tensing up somewhat as I usually do, I said to Malika, "This is going to be the best Ramadan ever!" Hopeful perhaps more than prescient, but it somehow deepened the intention we make for the fast, positivising the attitudinal music as it were, for indeed it did turn out that way for us.

And remembering the Ramadan of 1986, in Santa Barbara, when I made an intention to write a poem each day or night, and the month produced, by Allah, the book known as *Ramadan Sonnets*, I wondered if I might do the same now in 2011. But this year I heeded a remark once made to me by dear Syrian friend, writer and publisher Munir Akash, when I wrote the introduction to the first printed edition he published with City Lights of that book, that Arab readers at least would be less inclined to read my poems if they knew they came from rational intention rather than naked inspiration. Although it was truly that way for me when I wrote them, this time I made no formal intention, but only let the thought ride vaguely but buzzingly inside. And the result was that I did "receive" a poem each day or night of Ramadan, mostly unbidden, and with the new web immediacy that wasn't available in 1986, posted each new poem (or in two cases poems) for the day of the fast with audio readings of each one on my poetry blog, www.ecstaticxchange.wordpress.com.

This book is those poems, in the chronological order in which they were received, and for the days designated by their dates of composition. They run a modest gamut of formalities, mostly "open field" couplets, with a rhymed poem, a narrative fable, and a spider poem of direct observation (and she's still there at the writing of this introduction, lounging in her crazy nets), among others.

Ramadan is such a slice of timelessness into time for us fasters, and a doorway to such miraculous moments throughout its rigors, and has about it a personality of its own from Allah and His attendant angelic forces and prophetic miracles, that we are all propelled forward in its raw sunlight, burnished by our nighttime devotions and our faithful daytime fasting. These are not litanies for prayer, nor traditional Ramadan observances, perhaps, but fresh arrivals from my experience of fasting, as I look forward to an even longer summer day next year at Ramadan time (with yes a bit of trepidation as always), and hopefully a few more treasure-troves to come, insha'Allah, with God's blessing on all of us.

One time when the Shaikh came to Tus, the people entreated him to speak before an assembly. The Shaikh consented. At dawn a platform was set up in the Kanaqah of the Master and people began arriving and seating themselves. When the Shaikh came forth, the chanters recited from the Qor'an.

Meanwhile, so many people had come in that there was no more room left. The master of ceremonies rose to his feet and said: "May God have mercy on each person who takes one step forward from where he is."

The Shaikh exclaimed: "God bless Mohammad and his family, one and all!" And the Shaikh drew his hand down over his face and said: "Everything I wished to say and everything the prophets declared has just been said: 'May you advance one step from what you are.'"

And the Shaikh didn't say another word but came down from the platform and with that he brought the assembly to a close.

— Shaykh Abu Sa'id Abi'l-Kheyr,
(from *The Secrets of God's Mystical Oneness*)

FIRST NIGHT OF RAMADAN

A single stone is thrown in
and the canyon resounds with the

hallelujahs of angels

A single breath contains the
known and unknown universes

Back behind edgeless
space are motions that

vibrate the heart

Back behind ancient mountains and
historical intricacies

a shadow gives way to Light that has a
door in it to

let us through

We take no step that
doesn't bring us nearer

One sip and the oceans disappear

One glance and the skies
bend closer to hear our

emptiness

One heart-wrench elegant elevation
and we're on a

plateau tossing a stone in the dark
that never stops echoing

8/1
1 Ramadan

FOUR CORNERS OF THE UNIVERSE

The four corners of the universe
can be seen as a little room

deep inside the universe with
planetary motions out each window

as we sit in the center of the room
fasting or eating

A giant phoenix in dazzling glory
carries it through space

or not
as you wish

Solid on a flat earth solid as rock?
But definitely

flying through space

like it or not
whether we fast or eat

live or die
go on after death or end up

dry bones bereft of souls

Flames lick around us

or a tall forest of sunflowers

sparrows chasing sparrows
through their ragged stalks

skylarks looping above in the
sky above us

The Kaba is a four cornered
room in the universe

Our Kaba hearts are
rooms in the universe

planetary motions out each window
and in their frames

faces of benevolence
waiting for our cycles of

fasting and eating to become

one lifting of our hungry
hands held out palms up

for planetary motions
to fill them

with splashes of original amber

8/2
2 Ramadan

ADAM STOOD IN THE WORLD

Adam stood in the world
as tall as the trees

the sun bathing his body
birds wreathing his outline with

birdsong
waters everywhere splashing

growls and grandeur of new animals
ache of new growths everywhere

sounding

Alone he stood with a
hunger in his heart reaching out to

touch the edible nothingness
around him

His own essence before his
birth in Allah's domain

nourished on Light and the Names he'll
name creation with

to keep each radiant thing linked to
Allah's single simultaneous

action in the unseen

each kind of leaf made consciousness
each cloud in passing also conscious

each Adam-named element
dimensionalizing the world

and the angels

all on prophet Adam's
fasting tongue

articulating even
now if we bend in

close to our hearts to hear
that original

soft sound

                                                            8/3
                                                3 Ramadan

LEAVE THE WORLD ALONE

Sumptuous Juggler God Coy Beloved
Elusive Letter-writer from a distant land

beyond moonbeams and tides though You
send them to us enwrapped and encoded

in message bottles of their outer crusts
we must crack to comprehend or at least

hold up to ears like shells to hear Your
Voice resounding in a coral coil to the

infinitely minute central spiral whose nub is a
miracle dot from which the whole unfolds

again and again before us comprehensible
incomprehensible in dots and dashes

or among saintly ones in full flashes of
stupendous Light in a circular

cosmos of sun and moon and planetary
pastures filled with the Kingdom of the Animals

from which we rise enraptured of Your
Perfect Face —

we fast for You
and leave the world alone

8/4
4 Ramadan

BLACK COW RAMADAN

At our night of *dhikr* last night our
shaykh asked us what Ramadan is to each

one of us personally and
insisted that we not answer with

fancy platitudes embroidering
this and that but go deep and

come up with a true response

And I suddenly remembered one very dark
night nearly fifty years ago walking with a

friend on a pitch-black road back from a
village in Mexico to where we were

staying in Ajijic

No moon not a star in the sky
and we knew the

road well so we were walking along at a
brisk pace when suddenly

WHAM! I hit something
flat in my chest that

stopped me cold as if I'd walked into a

solid wall

Black cow invisible in the night crossing the
road right in front of me

that I could barely make out even after
squinting my eyes

until I reached out and
felt its passing hairy bulk

The fast of Ramadan
puts us up against it

Against our mortality our daily
existence on earth our *nafs*

No more fancy talk

only Allah

                                                8/5
                                          5 Ramadan

A FLOURISH OF TIME

A flourish of time and a life is complete
with its circles and straight lines

somehow converging at a
vanishing point

attended by woolen-clad angels awhirl in
blue ponds of vertical air

singing songs of ancient traditions and
neighboring galaxies beyond

human translation

yet we know their crystalline meanings
if not here and now at least in

far-off echoes past those hills in
distant outline where

other suns shine and other
moons catch their silvery rays

8/6
6 Ramadan

A FIERY GLOW IN THE HEART

Taste the nothing that isn't
and the nothingness that is

How many giraffes could gallop through those
words with their incredible vertical lope?

The nothing that isn't sounds like a
glove that if you pull it on your whole

body disappears to
pop up elsewhere

looking back at you through an
enormous window

The closer we get the
quieter it gets around us

I think whales understand this
moving through the deeps

We have these mouths and
digestive tracts through which the

world in all its dazzle passes

though we bite empty air

The joy of breaking the fast is

the meeting with our Lord

my Lord and your Lord

in an open plain with a
warm wind

as we pull on that glove and
disappear

Great yellow flowers bloom in the
trees and a golden road

undulates toward the X
where our destiny is fulfilled

biting empty air
turned inside-out around us

A catch of stars on the
roof of the house

a fiery glow
in the heart

8/7
7 Ramadan

SPLENDID EXCITEMENT OF THE COMING DAY

Splendid excitement of the coming day!

Palaces might await us filled with
the tangiest grapes

down esplanades of golden cypresses
behind walls we can

barely see over at dawn for the
height of their occasional distractions

But melodious lute music from a
hidden courtyard exudes

fragrant strums that
invite our hungry hearts to float past

their rough material stones

OK it's a day of fasting whose
treasures remain unseen

but we can almost feel the
spatial pressure to let them burst and

unload over us as the day progresses

and though their
gold may be nontransferable on the

common market

already the gurgle of flashing rivers of love's coins
delights our ears

and their deeper wealth entices us

Oh that sumptuous dazzling palace before us!
Wild festivities jingle-jangle there!

Endless dancing of heavenly bodies!

No breath taken that isn't
Allah's Name in a taste of

majestic succulence!

8/8
8 Ramadan

THE THINGS OF THIS WORLD

The things of this world have
gone a remove while fasting

as if through a kind of glazed window just
out of reach

which is where they always are though we
clutch their ghosts to us in a

curious waltz and
hope for the best

Ramadan casts its star-like
light making things stand out in

sharp relief from an
even starrier background

releasing us in His Mercy from their
clankier chains

8/9
9 Ramadan

RAMADAN IS BURNISHED SUNLIGHT

Ramadan is burnished sunlight on the
cheek of the Beloved at the

first dawn of creation

first fruits burst on first green
branches in the first Garden

their ripening a whole
lunar month without being picked

till they burst with the
celestial pleasure of pure being

Ramadan hunkers down in the extreme
depths of heaven and earth

simultaneously

as deep in the earth as the sky
bound together with immaterial

coils in the
knot of our fleshly hunger

It's a luminous door down a long hall in a
yearly wall in space

past rooms of resplendent solitudes and

incantatory gatherings with a

vision at the end of a tall silver stag whose
antlers are flames lighting our

way to inconceivable pastures
where endless bounty abounds

A weighty touch from an emptiness that
strikes sparks in our hearts

a turning from one light to another
even brighter than ocular radiance

Lick the tongue of it with our tongues!

Clear the throat of it with our throats!

Surround the sight of it in a blind blizzard of
overpouringness into our

suddenly increased dimension
as we stand a bit shakily at His

window
praising His Name

8/10
10 Ramadan

HIS PURE PRESENCE

A goat eats grass off the Beloved's hill
and gives white milk to the Beloved's Messenger

O body of seemingly little worth
discarded at our entrance to the

truer life
you are our road to Light troubled or

at ease

pockmarked with road-ruts or
smooth as Sahara dunes

and though we leave you behind

how precious we've been born in you
and travel in your

rubbery vehicle
on hidden bone tracks

to moment after moment of
space-time perfection

in an eyeblink

here one minute
the next minute

spatial

our gaze unceasing over all

*The Prophet came among us
grew to manhood*

died

*yet his pure presence is as palpable
as space itself*

Having drunk the milk we
drink each day

giving up food and drink
for a moon-cycle

for God's sweet sake alone

8/11
11 Ramadan

RAMADAN'S FLAME HOOPS

OK let's get this straight —

Who wants to fast really?

Put the body through drought's
grinding chains?

Not reach for the plum or the chocolate
bonbon?

When we see a Chinese contortionist and
think *how can she put her head onto*

*her feet like that without her spine
snapping* and that we might also think

and why?

Or a lion capable of
snapping the head off the spangled

guy with the whip
but instead roars and

leaps through a fiery hoop?

How close did the
spangled guy have to get to having his

head bitten off before

perfecting that smooth
sleek slow motion leap through flames to the

pit orchestra's brassy flourish?

It's a hard life we make even
harder by submitting to not eating for

nearly sixteen hours of normal
daylight?

But such a curious
turnabout happens when it's in a

dimension obligatory to Allah that truly
boggles the reluctant mind

in that a kind of garden does
open its pearl-handled gate in a

space that suddenly
imposes itself all during that

time and our
mortality actually always

hanging by a thread becomes
really quite incandescent!

I mean
crowded with

angels
known or unbeknownst to us

It so often
seems so

Our reluctant lion roars and we
put our heads on our feet

somehow passing through
Ramadan's flame hoops

with ease

                                                            8/12
                                                       12 Ramadan

SIGNS OF ALLAH

When the tide of the day pulls out and
leaves the night standing on the shore

swallowing the stars

and the moon is nearly halfway to
completing its luminous shell

and the night stretches its arms to
expand as far as the

globe's curvature will allow
with the sun's spotlight lighting up where

night is not and the night
darkening to the hazy line between them

and we take all this into our
bodies with the daytime fast

are we not now inhabiting a space that is
neither exactly terrestrial nor celestial

but by the decree of prophetic consciousness
participating as we might otherwise not

in the in and out breathing of Allah's most
essential creating?

We see the signs of Allah on the
horizons of heaven and earth

and they are

ourselves

>8/14
>14 Ramadan

RAMADAN GOES LOOKING

Ramadan goes looking for the
people who fast the best

wearing the phases of the moon
as a shield upon its breast

ignoring stars and galaxies
as too far out in space

concentrating instead
on light in a faster's face

or if a face is darkened
what is passing through the heart

of someone who resists the world
for this month so set apart

It goes to the best and worst places
looking for a perfect one

who finds the diamond of Ramadan
flashing in the daytime sun

High and low it searches
among the elegant and the poor

who put aside food and drink
to stand in Allah's corridor

awaiting entrance to His precincts
where finer delicacies are served

who spend their days in fasting
and never think to swerve

It climbs to mountain caves
and sits with hermit saints

and sees illumined worlds in eyes
no words can ever paint

of nearness by Allah's tight blessing
on the hearts of His bosom friends

who've left all vestiges of matter
for nourishment that never ends

But then it sees a glimmer
not far off at all

in the deep intention of everyone
to fulfill the Prophet's call

that shines in the heart of our hearts
and is the diamond *behind* that shine

to endure hardship for Allah's sake
however simple or sublime

And sees in its faceted perfection

every faster's face

on the surface of that diamond
out of all time and space

in the answer to Allah's call
to turn to Him alone

before everything we so love in the world
turns to stone

8/14
14 Ramadan

HAND OF LIGHT

A crater opens in the day
and swallows us whole

Though we may want to
wander at the base of it

asking for water
we do not

Instead we lean back against its diamonds
and act nonchalant

Inside us huge circular processions
flow around God's cubical House

They are incessant and
no one seems to mind

In fact each one of them is
ascending a diamond mountain so

near Allah's intimate Hearing they
brush against the unspeakable

tenderness there that makes even
stones weep

This is a time like no other

We wouldn't barter it for the world

If the world knew its worth they would
demand its largesse in even

larger quantities and
pay for it with their lives

Perhaps it's a
secret kept pure by being

kept secret

Yet its essence is no secret at all
but so well known every citizen alive

vibrates heartfully at its deep harmonious
core

one month of the Moon
in its death and rebirth to clear silver

no one escaping from God's
hand of Light passing over them

to set them free into the

captivity of His love

8/15
15 Ramadan

HALFWAY THROUGH THE FAST

Halfway through the fast
is it a giant granite stone we shoulder

uphill in a boiling sun?

Or pool after reflective shady
pool in fragrant afternoons that

flow everywhere?

Is it coming face to face with
ourselves holding an empty

walnut shell in a
cubicle of mirrors

or suddenly relieved of the
anatomical discomforts of our

egos' slouches and shrugs we think
define us

now we sit as easy as
weightless jockeys on

horses of burnished silver
for the race to the finish?

The universe surrounds us with a
personable hug

that with days of
gastronomical emptiness we sense the

deft butterfly touch that actually
makes up its doings and

goings

Allah's subtlety in the
interconnectedness of all things

as our beings move forward while others
sail past in the opposite

way but go to the exact
same place in His dazzling

geometrical perfection

these close-ups of shattered and
reshaped patterns pouring their

diamond endlessness all around us
Light upon

irrefutable
Light

8/15
15 Ramadan

THE CAPITULATION OF KING STOMACH

Slave stomach said to the
rest of the body *"I am King!"*

and the general populace of the
body acquiesced worried lest

its bond with the world be
broken without stomach holding

a sovereign position over the
rest of its territories limbs thoughts

dreams desires ambitions successes
at least in this world if not in the

next

So King Stomach sat on a huge corpuscle
throne counting calories and

balancing proteins and carbohydrates like
so many vassals made to

till King Stomach's fields and bring in
his bounteous harvests

Soon the body's bond was tighter than
ever with the things of this

world and King Stomach began to
lust after ever greater power

taking over traditional villages and cities with

tacky McDonalds and pre-fab Pizza Huts

everywhere on this good green earth making people
once so sensitive now somewhat fat and lazy

Then one day outside the palace
a procession with an army of angels preceding it

came to the gates asking for an
audience with the king

The angelic army on camels beneficently benign
protecting a palanquin of purest mist

that shielded a greater monarch asking for entrance to the
body's domain

Queen Ramadan come to request a single favor by the
light of the glowing sliver of the new moon

King Stomach looked out his high turreted window
and quailed in his ten gallon gastronomical boots

for coming to see him was a
reflected radiance so intense it could

dissolve resistance with a
single glance

weakening King Stomach's hold and
replacing it with a still tasty but less

obsessively bottled-up appetite

The palanquin of mist entered as if swallowing and

Queen Ramadan in all her invisible regalia

faced King Stomach with a moon face of
unutterable beauty

eyelids of bougainvillea landscapes
cheeks of exotic Samarkand roses

lips of Granadan pomegranates with
highlights of oranges from Seville

aromas even greater than the palace
kitchen on feast days and a

delicate embrace the king felt surrounding his
gargantuan but now vulnerable dimensions

He could feel his conquered lands
shrinking before his eyes and the

bondage of multitudes lifting as
Queen Ramadan asked for only

one month a year to maintain her Spartan dominion
which King Stomach falling under her spell

granted in spite of his initial and once deeply
entrenched reluctance

and with his decree now made into law

the whole body prospered to the
utmost extent of its thoughts and limbs

and spiritual latitudes unfolded in

lotus level after glorious level and chrysanthemum

cloud after resplendent cloud and
vegetable step after deep earthly step toward the

high trumpet blasts of a
greater and more delicious

interior Garden of Delights than even
King Stomach in all his

tyrannical pomp
could ever possibly

envision

8/17
17 Ramadan

A SPIDER'S BREAK-FAST

The small brown spider in my bathroom
(honored guest whose

protection is assured)
after more than two weeks of patient waiting

finally got a large tasty black fly-like
bug this morning in her

helter-skelter-looking web (to
me at least) linked to a retracting

mirror and the wall near a
nightlight I keep on so she perhaps

likes the dim glow and mild heat

And all through the night she spent
wrapping and sucking out the

goodness and turning and turning the trapped
big bug around in her legs

and this morning at dawn as well she was
still rotating it in her

spidery fashion but when I
peered at her just now past noon

no trace of bug remained (pitiful
remnants on the floor below?) but my

lady spider's abdomen bulges elegantly

round so she's no doubt now

dreaming away and digesting her
sweet feast in whatever consciousness a

spider has or needs and is probably
sated enough for now to await the

next morsel as patiently as she
must

8/18
18 Ramadan

EXTEND YOUR SHADOW

If you haven't been parted from
what you truly love

then foot cannot follow foot
nor heart follow heart

Beasts born in the wild have the
wild to bring them to

their higher education

How can we see what
will wire us to bring us

to the deep circuitry of
God's illumination?

None but Ahmad the Radiant One
peace be upon him

casts no shadow

Shall we cut away our shadows to
stride from them in the Prophet's

shadowless domain?

Or embrace our luscious darknesses
to both tame and extend their

shapely union?

The sun in each galaxy

is the central teacher

across this edgeless universe
of myriad circumferences

each sun the single pivot who
binds each orbit to its

divinely turning dances

and the tilt of its orbs
is each one's consequences

Though the Prophet had the moon's face
his Light was that of the sun

Oh Shams of all time to come!

In our own hearts galactic wheels
are turning

and the sound of melodic sighing
fills our ears with its burning

and its song of separation
fills our yearning

For everyone God's departure has
never taken place —

*Extend your shadow to become
the incandescence of His Face*

8/19
19 Ramadan

WITH A TWO-LEGGED GOAT AND A FLYING FISH

Who I've become after all my
adventures on land

is a seventy-one year-old man who
fasts from dawn to sundown

sailing off across the day
with a two-legged goat and a

flying fish searching for the
source of all this daylight

avoiding the usual ports of call
in favor of sleepy villages where

everyone knows everyone's name and
night rolls its huge velvet

blanket over the rooftops of the
satisfied and satisfactory villagers

If I meet you once I'll remember your
face forever

but your name might roll back into the
Babylonian directory of ghostly mortals

And if you see me in one place you'll maybe
see me in another as

likely as a face appearing from
inside an iceberg

or a song audible in a
light spring rainfall

This is all coming right out of nowhere
and like all of us goes right

back where it came from
though at the end of the day when

plates are filled with rainbow
meats and Technicolor juices

and the tattooed sails are
mended for tomorrow and the

goat hobbles onto evening pastures
and the flying fish finally finds a

plot of water to plop in

you'll see celebration in my eyes
of all these seventy-one years

come to fruition

and *"God be praised!"* on my lips
even if cracked by the many minor

hardships endured

8/20
20 Ramadan

RAMADAN SUNS ITSELF

Ramadan suns itself by the dark of night
and takes no notice of

earthquake or flood

Ramadan begins walking toward us from the
furthest hilltop of the previous year

and arrives at our door with
baskets of golden fruit

Although Ramadan seems most at home in
lavish "oriental" settings of jeweled

ewers and plashing fountains
our faces can best be reflected in its

battered tin plates and small sheltered ponds

No one has ever disappeared into Ramadan
never to be seen again

or if they do they appear again at the
Festival in bright silvery clothes

handing out sweets wrapped in our
most personal names

Ramadan is the most patient among us
and endures our anxieties with

perfect poise
never turning its face away

If we knew the treasures of Ramadan we would
want the fast to take place every

day of the year

but the sparkling gold of its coins dissolves into
denominational numbers when

Ramadan ends

If Ramadan were a horse it would be
a herd of the finest thoroughbreds

and each of us would be assigned the one most
suited to our variable temperaments

Ramadan is an ocean that waits each year in a
dimension of space and when it

bursts onto shore it
inundates our souls having transformed our

slightest actions into flying doves

Ramadan ends the way it begins
silently and with the

deepest humility

leaving through the same front door
through which it came

When the Prophet tightens his belt for
Ramadan each of us feels it

some losing and some gaining
the weight of its privations

Love arrives in the disguise of Ramadan
and when it removes its mask we find

it's been with us all along
as familiar to us as

ourselves

but more than we were before

and less

8/21
21 Ramadan

PINPOINT AND COMPASS POINT

A pinpoint and a compass point
a *bismin* and a galaxy

What do they have in common?

A cloud in the sky and a thought passing
through our heads with maybe even

more wind behind it

A single wave in the sea folding over and
under the great watery vastness and our

lives deeper than even the
darkest depths of its phosphorescent

darkness

with even more dazzling cosmos in them to all its
farthest reaches and most

specifically particular details though we

continue on past cosmos after all to where both
the edges and the actual edgelessness of this gorgeous

spectral universe no longer matter

and leaves the size of planets wave in
other-than-planetary breezes and rivers of a

water so sweet and fine flow to that
disappearing ocean of our mortality that

empties into even greater
waters of immortality as

defined by the promised sent Prophet to us
from The Sender of all prophets and

inspirations through time and to all
humankind out of time linking

pinpoints and counterpoints
compass points and *bismins*

sunrises and twilight
freedom from tyrants

and bright green skies that link these
worlds above all

in God's most shiny and most
beauteous reflection of His

most Majestic
Face

8/22
22 Ramadan

FAST

Puppets can't break their fast
through their painted mouths

Rocks can be said to be
fasting forever

Mountain "fastnesses" are a kind of
stronghold or fortress

Colors are fast that never
cut and run

The Ramadan fast goes by day by
sometimes-uphill-day anything but

fast

though if we fasten ourselves to it
it seems to go faster

and with an "e" thrown in for
"effort" we can look

forward to a *feast*

and so faithfully fulfill our
fast

8/22
22 Ramadan

HEART & SOUL

If all my poems seem to end up in the
same place it's because I

also want to end up there
grateful to God and

showered by the bliss of His Face

Starting from a shadow say cast by an
alleyway in Chinatown on a dark

Wednesday or off a ship say in Nova Scotia
smelling of codfish and sea brine or

landing in Rome hoping to visit the
languorous green vineyards of Tuscany

but moving forward in the time left to us
which might be decades or ten seconds only

each footstep a compass point pinpoint on our
still unrolling map with its

expectancies and definite concisions
leaving some slack time or clenching it

tighter for God's own utterly precise
pinpointed compass pointing

to which we can only happily concede

always going with His sweet Will and
little of our own with eyes open and

His name and deep destination
always on our lips heart and soul

or when we suddenly remember having
momentarily dreamed our little life away

to get back to it

with forward lunge and straight shot
heading out both heart and soul to seek

His fortune and its plenitudes and
none of our own or only

as much of "our own" as will
help in the project

to get us there

8/23
23 Ramadan

RAMADAN IS A GORGEOUS CHORUS

Ramadan is a gorgeous chorus
repeated in a mist above glades of

green wheat bending in blue light

Ramadan meets itself coming in from
the rain with its face slick and shining

and sits at our table as it vanishes with all its
viands back into pure spirit set with

foaming golden goblets of Paradise

A warm breeze aromatic with jasmine
rises around our bodies as we

pass between miles of monotone graves on our
way to Eternity's low doorway

A fountain appears in the middle of
everything and in its splashing music

proclaims exactly why we endure the
fast and how He will embrace us

on the other side in the
sweet exhaustion of our endurance

Scrolls of fire turn into waterfalls of
ice in the air all around us

each with our own particular wisdom

as the world sets like a planet under the
moon's horizon of our lunar month

and we let its ribbons and streamers
go as it pursues its worldly parade

up to cliff-edge after cliff-edge of seemingly
unavoidable disaster

Ramadan has freed us and it's for
us to remain in this concentrated

state now for Allah's sake alone
eating the grapes of unity and sipping

its wine in every weather of
satisfaction with His

impeccable Decree

8/24
24 Ramadan

IF WE WOKE UP ONE MORNING

If we woke up one morning to find
we didn't exist

would the fast be abrogated?

Or be more completely fulfilled?

If we were a
vague fractal outline among mountain crags or

mounded clouds

or mingled in aromatic breezes through
maple leaves in an

urban backyard whose branches lean
over a back alley fence

or a silence among howls of wolves
or the screeching of bus brakes

and we existed only as a peaceable serenity in a
transparent atmosphere that could

take place anywhere anytime on earth

watching through eyes God watches through
into the poignant brutalities of His

creation as well as its upsurging and
overpoweringly intense Light through it all

and we were here but not here just as

Ramadan's four or more invisible dimensions

slide down into our lives in time and almost
make us non-existent in a

strange way with sharper sensitivities to
the fall of each sparrow or birth of each

moth who lands on our bathroom
mirror and suddenly

doubles itself facing itself where
before there was none

and we
see it land in its

bright fragile beauty
and are amazed

8/25
25 Ramadan

BLUE CIRCLES

Tell again the story of how you saw the
two blue circles rhyme

as in a circus

and how the ground was wet and the
light hard to see by

and how a zebra loomed out of the
shadows and

caught you off guard as you
walked past the rotating bird

One night of the year when
God is so close you can almost see a

breath along the ground that
can't be explained any other way

than divine
and the animals grow still

and the quiet becomes a
dimension in which we dwell

That night like no other
showing the worth of our waiting

and what we are made of
nothing we can quantify

of a worth whose worthlessness we

cannot estimate and a

worthlessness whose every one of us
is monarch of our little space

where God dwells and king becomes
slave to live in pure

mathematical harmony
with His self-erasing Infinity

enough light for the

blind tightrope walker to sing as she
crosses to the other side

above us

8/25
25 Ramadan

NIGHTTIME SESSIONS OF LIGHT

*for Baji (who heard the geese
calling out Allah Allah)*

Intense nighttime sessions of Light
spangle the planetary air and the

lunar crescendo *yup* I said the

lunar crescendo as we
head toward Ramadan's exit back into

temptation's roundelay *yup* I said

temptation's roundelay that seems to go round and
round though for one blessed

month a year we step off it whether it
grinds to a halt or goes off its

spiraling pivot with sparks
screeching the asphalt as in

"Strangers on a Train" that
catastrophic carousel atilt in extremity

for all Eternity

But a crystally nighttime dome appears and we
look out onto blessed Blakean moonlight

and daytime geese across the sky above us
honk the Divine Name as

clearly as can be as they head toward
Canada in a fine summer rain

and we're back on earth again

8/26
26 Ramadan

THE REPETITIONS OF SAINTS

for Bawa Muhaiyuddeen (et al.)

The repetitions of saints flow through every
leaf and glisten hanging by threads from

branches of Divine Breath interwoven

in the universe's big starry basket tilted in His
burning Glance and suspended by His

cool ocular steadiness throughout time to tip out
lively bubbles of intensest Grace in

which we live and that live in us for
all time to come as we

slide through the billion worlds by the pulse of those
repetitions heartbeat by heartbeat in the

saints' huge bodies
thinner than a hair

held aloft for a nanosecond
in the air

I sit near the saint's empty bed in his
green room where so many angels make for

barely enough elbow-space so
tightly packed angelic

elbow to elbow and
wing to incandescent wing

and everything's become a giant ear
on a wave rising perceptibly entrance-ward

to God's perfect everywhere

8/26
26 Ramadan

IRENE

A raindrop big as a small
country is landing on our back garden

a powerful fragment at a time then
running in a fast moving runnel down the

back alley and all this even before
Hurricane Irene hits with full force

and as Irene means *"peace"* so
"Good Night Irene" as the

old song says may you
turn away from our shore and

dizzy yourself

out at sea somewhere to a
merriment of dolphins and a wild

spinning of silent dervish creatures of the
deeps *Oh Allah!* Preserve us from Your

watery Wrath that we might
see Your Might of Power with

humility

and flow in runnels with Your Perfect
Calm

a wall of water we walk through to Your
pure oasis

as the night wears on

8/27
27 Ramadan

AT THE PIVOT END OF A LIFE

At the pivot end of a life
(between this world and the next)

all the sleek black horses lined up for
inspection

all the torn and tattered love letters tied in their
appropriate bundles

and the words we've left in the air like
washing hanging out to dry

(some come back to us having been
happily stretched and whitened while others

track us down with yeah sad and
unsightly stains)

At the turning point where the
dark woods ahead begin to take

shape showing deeper and deeper shadows and
sharper contrasts

and the miles of galleries behind us with our
finger-paintings hung straight or hopelessly

askew are suddenly
neon lit

And at the poignant points of gratitude after
hurricane or flood earthquake or

Dracula-threat that turns out to be
nothing after all but

incessant mouse-squeaks

and we find ourselves high and dry in His Mercy as
usual with a

strong wind blowing through our clothes
and our breaths more mixed now with the

singsong melodies of the surrounding air
on both purple-shadowy mountain peak or

front porch on a couch with spouse in a
delicious downpour

But the pivot-point anytime anywhere
at any point

and the long or short lines of well-wishers
are everyone or no one as the death woods

open up doorways between trees and show
shadows both luscious and soberingly frightening

one step ahead of us with our
one foot still firm where we are in life

and the other tentatively raised for
forward movement

waiting a moment for the upsurge in our
hearts to show us which way ahead to go

(and ahead the
best place willingly or unwillingly

to go)

And this poem has no way of ending except this
pivot point in expectant tightrope

suspension between
this world with its presumed

finalities and the
next with its personal

Godly apocalypse somewhat
domesticated for use

at the constant and immediate
swivelingly bewildered and

drunkenly reflective

  pivot end of a life

8/28
28 Ramadan

ELUSIVE CRESCENT

Ah coy crescent hiding in a blush of sky
so many want to see you and

hold you to our hearts
each in our own perimeters however

spread across the earth all searching
for your quick eyeblink that promises

untold bounteous rewards for our
month of doing without in

obedience to first sighting you nearly
hidden as always in your rosy cheek of clouds

What a miracle! That there could be
only one of you when so many

hearts have mirrors extended skyward to reflect your
silvery light asliver with such slight

shiveriness and so soon
gone again below the curve of our brows

And why not many crescents in God's
Generous Splendor that not each

statue of us stand stock still on the

exact same spot of day but each of your
lovers has your breath upon our glass

a mist of love you sign your shy
name to

furtive in the sky

as we end our fast?

8/29
29 Ramadan

A SANDWICH AT NOON

A sandwich at noon is enough to
frighten a field of crows

A telephone ringing in an empty room is
answered by the wind

A road leading upward has a
bicycle on it and two trees

When the blessings were brought in
the sun rolled to a stop

Going past the stables all the black horses
flared their nostrils at once

The month of light was sealed and sent to its
Divine Recipient the year we

lived in trees and
sang at dawn

There's a stubbornness in refusing to flow
out the gate onto the fresh fields of

clover and recently turned pasturage

The celebration began when the moon
turned into a table set with

silver utensils and Samarkand oranges

Rainbows seemed to fill every window
from multiple light sources

The room spun around while we
remained still but it never went

faster than the earth's rotation
and the spiraling stars

Young girl acrobats stood on
each other's shoulders almost reaching

the moon

Daylight fills every corner and awakens
the mouse family

Grandpa told this in story form and it
all cohered

But today is another day and the
dolphins have all departed

back to their pods

Does the earth revolve toward us or
away from us?

Does the sky pass behind us
or ahead of us?

Take a step in any direction
and you're home

where the celebration continues
until dawn though the

rooster may not crow it open

flopping his red crown

I've covered a lot of ground sitting here
and don't intend to correct it

I try not to be out with my sheep
when God visits my hovel

but the north side of the mountain gets chilled
before a fire can be properly stoked

I hear a buzz of words in the air
mixed with a buzz of insects and the

usual high frequency buzz in my ears
I take as celestial music

Deciphering is all we do and we do it
best in our sleep

I greet anyone intrepid enough to speak
and anyone foolhardy enough to listen

It's over now
The dawn is up

A new day's begun

8/30
30 Ramadan (1 Shawwal)

INDEX

Author's Introduction 8

A Fiery Glow in the Heart 21
A Flourish of Time 20
A Sandwich at Noon 77
A Spider's Break-Fast 46
Adam Stood in the World 15
At the Pivot End of a Life 72
Black Cow Ramadan 18
Blue Circles 64
Elusive Crescent 75
Extend Your Shadow 48
Fast 57
First Night of Ramadan 11
Four Corners of the Universe 13
Halfway Through the Fast 40
Hand of Light 38
Heart & Soul 58
His Pure Presence 28
If We Woke Up One Morning 62
Irene 70
Leave the World Alone 17
Nighttime Sessions of Light 66
Pinpoint and Compass Point 55
Ramadan Goes Looking 35
Ramadan Suns Itself 52
Ramadan is Burnished Sunlight 26
Ramadan is a Gorgeous Chorus 60
Ramadan's Flame Hoops 30
Signs of Allah 33
Splendid Excitement of the Coming Day 23
The Capitulation of King Stomach 42
The Repetitions of Saints 68
The Things of this World 25
With a Two-Legged Goat and a Flying Fish 50

ABOUT THE AUTHOR

Born in 1940 in Oakland, California, Daniel Abdal-Hayy Moore had his first book of poems, *Dawn Visions*, published by Lawrence Ferlinghetti of City Lights Books, San Francisco, in 1964, and the second in 1972, *Burnt Heart/Ode to the War Dead*. He created and directed *The Floating Lotus Magic Opera Company* in Berkeley, California in the late 60s, and presented two major productions, *The Walls Are Running Blood*, and *Bliss Apocalypse*. He became a Sufi Muslim in 1970, performed the Hajj in 1972, and lived and traveled throughout Morocco, Spain, Algeria and Nigeria, landing in California and publishing *The Desert is the Only Way Out*, and *Chronicles of Akhira* in the early 80s (Zilzal Press). Residing in Philadelphia since 1990, in 1996 he published *The Ramadan Sonnets* (Jusoor/City Lights), and in 2002, *The Blind Beekeeper* (Jusoor/Syracuse University Press). He has been the major editor for a number of works, including *The Burdah* of Shaykh Busiri, translated by Hamza Yusuf, and the poetry of Palestinian poet, Mahmoud Darwish, translated by Munir Akash. He is also widely published on the worldwide web: *The American Muslim, DeenPort*, and his own website and poetry blog, among others: *www.danielmoorepoetry.com, www.ecstaticxchange.wordpress.com*. He has been poetry editor for *Seasons Journal, Islamica Magazine,* a 2010 translation by Munir Akash of *State of Siege*, by Mahmoud Darwish (Syracuse University Press), and *The Prayer of the Oppressed*, by Imam Muhammad Nasir al-Dar'i, translated by Hamza Yusuf. In 2011 he was a winner of the Nazim Hikmet Prize for Poetry. *The Ecstatic Exchange Series* is bringing out the extensive body of his works of poetry (a complete list of published works on page 2).

POETIC WORKS by Daniel Abdal-Hayy Moore
Published and Unpublished

Dawn Visions (published by City Lights, 1964)
Burnt Heart/Ode to the War Dead (published by City Lights, 1972)
This Body of Black Light Gone Through the Diamond (printed by Fred Stone, Cambridge, Mass, 1965)
On The Streets at Night Alone (1965?)
All Hail the Surgical Lamp (1967)
States of Amazement (1970)

Abdallah Jones and the Disappearing-Dust Caper (published by The Ecstatic Exchange/Crescent Series, 2006)
'Ala ud-Deen and the Magic Lamp
The Chronicles of Akhira (1981) (published by Zilzal Press with Typoglyphs by Karl Kempton, 1986; published in Sparrow on the Prophet's Tomb by The Ecstatic Exchange, 2009)
Mouloud (1984) (A Zilzal Press chapbook, 1995; published in Sparrow on the Prophet's Tomb by The Ecstatic Exchange, 2009)
Man is the Crown of Creation (1984)
The Look of the Lion (The Parabolas of Sight) (1984)
The Desert is the Only Way Out (completed 4/21/84) (Zilzal Press chapbook, 1985)
Atomic Dance (1984) (am here books, 1988)
Outlandish Tales (1984)
Awake as Never Before (12/26/84) (Zilzal Press chapbook, 1993)
Glorious Intervals (1/1/85) (Zilzal Press chapbook, ?)
Long Days on Earth/Book I (1/28 – 8/30/85)
Long Days on Earth/Book II (Hayy Ibn Yaqzan)
Long Days on Earth/Book III (1/22/86)
Long Days on Earth/Book IV (1986)
The Ramadan Sonnets (Long Days on Earth/Book V) (5/9 – 6/11/86) (published by Jusoor/City Lights Books, 1996) (republished as Ramadan Sonnets by The Ecstatic Exchange, 2005)
Long Days on Earth/Book VI (6-8/30/86)
Holograms (9/4/86 – 3/26/87)
History of the World (The Epic of Man's Survival) (4/7 – 6/18/87)
Exploratory Odes (6/25 – 10/18/87)

The Man at the End of the World (11/11 – 12/10/87)
The Perfect Orchestra (3/30 – 7/25/88)(published by The Ecstatic Exchange, 2009)
Fed from Underground Springs (7/30 – 11/23/88)
Ideas of the Heart (11/27/88 – 5/5/89)
New Poems (scattered poems, out of series, from 3/24 – 8/9/89)
Facing Mecca (5/16 – 11/11/89)
A Maddening Disregard for the Passage of Time (11/17/89 – 5/20/90) (published by The Ecstatic Exchange, 2009)
The Heart Falls in Love with Visions of Perfection (6/15/90 – 6/2/91)
Like When You Wave at a Train and the Train Hoots Back at You (Farid's Book) (6/11 – 7/26/91) (published by The Ecstatic Exchange, 2008)
Orpheus Meets Morpheus (8/1/91– 3/14/92)
The Puzzle (3/21/92 – 8/17/93)(published by The Ecstatic Exchange, 2011)
The Greater Vehicle (10/17/93 – 4/30/94)
A Hundred Little 3-D Pictures (5/14/94 – 9/11/95)
The Angel Broadcast (9/29 – 12/17/95)
Mecca/Medina Time-Warp (12/19/95 – 1/6/96) (published as a Zilzal Press chapbook, 1996)(published in Sparrow on the Prophet's Tomb, 2009)
Miracle Songs for the Millennium (1/20 – 10/16/96)
The Blind Beekeeper (11/15/96 – 5/30/97) (published 2002 by Jusoor/Syracuse University Press)
Chants for the Beauty Feast (6/3 – 10/28/97)(published by The Ecstatic Exchange, 2011
You Open a Door and it's a Starry Night (10/29/97 – 5/23/98) (published by The Ecstatic Exchange, 2009)
Salt Prayers (5/29 – 10/24/98) (published by The Ecstatic Exchange, 2005)
Some (10/25/98 – 4/25/99)
Flight to Egypt (5/1 – 5/16/99)
I Imagine a Lion (5/21 – 11/15/99) (published by The Ecstatic Exchange, 2006)
Millennial Prognostications (11/25/99 – 2/2/2000) (published by the Ecstatic Exchange, 2009)
Shaking the Quicksilver Pool (2/4 – 10/8/2000) (published by The Ecstatic Exchange, 2009)
Blood Songs (10/9/2000 – 4/3/2001)
The Music Space (4/10 – 9/16/2001) (published by The Ecstatic Exchange, 2007)

Where Death Goes (9/20/2001 – 5/1/2002) (published by The Ecstatic Exchange, 2009)

The Flame of Transformation Turns to Light (99 Ghazals Written in English) (5/14 – 8/21/2002) (published by The Ecstatic Exchange, 2007)

Through Rose-Colored Glasses (7/22/2002 – 1/15/2003) (published by The Ecstatic Exchange, 2007)

Psalms for the Broken-Hearted (1/22 – 5/25/2003) (published by The Ecstatic Exchange, 2006)

Hoopoe's Argument (5/27 – 9/18/03)

Love is a Letter Burning in a High Wind (9/21 – 11/6/2003) (published by The Ecstatic Exchange, 2006)

Laughing Buddha/Weeping Sufi (11/7/2003 – 1/10/2004) (published by The Ecstatic Exchange, 2005)

Mars and Beyond (1/20 – 3/29/2004) (published by The Ecstatic Exchange, 2005)

Underwater Galaxies (4/5 – 7/21/2004) (published by The Ecstatic Exchange, 2007)

Cooked Oranges (7/23/2004 – 1/24/2005 (published by The Ecstatic Exchange, 2007)

Holiday from the Perfect Crime (1/25 – 6/11/2005)(published by The Ecstatic Exchange, 2011)

Stories Too Fiery to Sing Too Watery to Whisper (6/13 – 10/24/2005)

Coattails of the Saint (10/26/2005 – 5/10/2006) (published by The Ecstatic Exchange, 2006)

In the Realm of Neither (5/14/2006 – 11/12/06) (published by The Ecstatic Exchange, 2008)

Invention of the Wheel (11/13/06 – 6/10/07)(published by The Ecstatic Exchange, 2010)

The Sound of Geese Over the House (6/15 – 11/4/07)

The Fire Eater's Lunchbreak (11/11/07 – 5/19/2008) (published by The Ecstatic Exchange, 2008)

Sparks Off the Main Strike (5/24/2008 – 1/10/2009)(published by The Ecstatic Exchange, 2010)

Stretched Out on Amethysts (1/13 – 9/17/2009)(published by The Ecstatic Exchange, 2010)

The Throne Perpendicular to All that is Horizontal (9/18/09 – 1/25/10)

In Constant Incandescence (2/10 – 8/13/10) (published by The Ecstatic Exchange, 2011)

The Caged Bear Spies the Angel (8/30/10 – 3/6/11)(published by The Ecstatic Exchange, 2010)
This Light Slants Upward (3/7/11 –)
Ramadan is Burnished Sunlight (part of This Light Slants Upward, published separately by The Ecstatic Exchange, 2011)